# You're the Right Mom for Your Kids

Bite-sized Pep Talks Just For You

by

Christy Thomas

Copyright © 2023 Christy Thomas
All rights reserved.
Published by Hoodie & Latte Books
Imprint of Honest Toddler Books
HonestToddlerBooks.com
ISBN: 978-0-9905928-8-4

All rights reserved. This book or any portion thereof may not be reproduced or used in any manner whatsoever without the express written permission of the publisher except for the use of brief quotations in a book review.

## DEDICATION

To my kids— Catherine, Lucia, and Lincoln may you never doubt you are loved with each breath you take. Even on the most challenging days
of motherhood you were always wanted. You are pure joy.

# Introduction

Dear Mom,

I don't know what prompted you to pick up this exact book, but I'm so glad you did.

Here's what I know to be true. You are exactly the right mom for your kids. You live in a society that values output more than nurturing. But your work as a mother is important.

There are days, maybe weeks or months, when you feel genuinely invisible to everyone except your children. And while those children are lovely, unique, one-of-a-kind miracles, they're also needy, physically and emotionally exhausting. That's why I'm here.

For a lot of us, motherhood is the most challenging, most rewarding of experiences in life.

You are the one who stays up late worrying and searching Google for symptoms. You are the one to nurture them when they are sick. You are the mother bear for them.

In that whirlwind experience of mothering, you can sometimes lose your identity- your ability to notice your own needs and feel isolated and lonely.

If you nodded along to the above, I wrote this book for you.

You are doing holy work and I see you.

I hope this book soothes you. I hope this book feels like a hand on your back and encourages you. After reading, I hope you feel safe enough to whisper to your friends on the hard days and tell them the truth.

I hope you let down your hair and remember that motherhood, while serious, doesn't need to be serious all the time.

**I hope you know you have always been precisely the right, good enough mom for your kids.**

I'm your Mary Poppins and Mr. Rogers cheering you along and holding your hand.

While I love kids, I love moms more. To me, you are the cornerstone of our communities and culture and protect everyone's future. Mothers are radically optimistic and breathe love into every action they do. As beacons of hope and drumbeats for home, we bring hope to the world.

You're the Right Mom For Your Kids

You are worthy of care and comfort. This book is meant precisely for you, and I am here to care for you, dear caregiver.

Love, Christy

# About the Author

My name is Christy. I am married to my college sweetheart who, along with others on submarines, hides underwater with no communication for months at a time in the US Navy. We have three wonderful children. They are three walking miracles who have helped me grow into a more compassionate and loving human being every day.

It has never been easy for me to be a mother. We've had quite a few unexpected hurdles. Through those experiences, I've learned self-compassion, mindfulness, and a type of mothering that sees me as a person with needs and priorities.

Being a Navy wife has been a wild ride and a remarkable story I could have never predicted.

In November 2018, we moved again to a new town where I didn't know anyone. On a whim, I recorded a podcast and uploaded it before we headed off to the children's science museum. When it started, it was called Everyday Motherhood. During the great shutdown of 2020, I changed the title to Keep Calm Mother On. Each episode has always ended with a self-care and family connection play idea. I wanted it to be practical and helpful: the voice I wish I had found when my husband was on his first deployment and I had two toddlers at home.

You don't need to read this book in one sitting. I wrote it knowing you have only one hand free most of the day. You can open the book randomly or read it like a novel. I know the right message will come to you.

Put your hand on your heart with me and breathe. You are doing a good enough job.

Don't give up. I'm shoulder to shoulder with you right now. I'm glad you're here.

XO

Christy Thomas

# You're the Right Mom for Your Kids

Bite-sized Pep Talks Just For You

You're the right mom for your kids. I do not doubt that it is true. You're a caring adult who has her heart in a knot. You care so much. It's not an accident or mistake. Your kid is lucky to have you. Your eyes light up when you see them before they see you. Your smile sneaks across your face when you say their name and share something that makes you laugh. Raising a human isn't easy—but you are the right mom for your kids.

# You're the Right Mom For Your Kids

Christy Thomas

Have you ever found a whole bottle of red glitter poured out on a wood floor with significant gaps between the planks? Maybe you haven't, but you can feel my pain, right? It was a beautiful mess. My toddler's fat feet danced in it, and she fell asleep with diamonds on her soles. What seemed like a horror show moment is now a sweet memory. Motherhood moves fast. Take a deep breath and know this will pass. You are so loved. Don't give up. You're not doing anything wrong.

## You're the Right Mom For Your Kids

My kids aren't perfect and every time I rediscover this it's a shock. When you have a baby, you have all these exquisite dreams of *perfect* and *wonderful*. Ten fingers, ten toes, and all that. My kids have developmental concerns, medical concerns, and mental health hurdles. When a new "flaw" is discovered, I wonder if I did something wrong when growing them. I didn't. I'm the right mom for this rag-tag bunch of perfect and beautiful oddities. They are perfect for me. Whatever your kids have as challenges—you're the right mom for that, too. Challenges are part of being human, so be excessively gentle with yourself. Because just like when you give a mouse a cookie, each new discovery will give you a unique gift of compassion. Never doubt that you're the right match. Lean on each other.

Christy Thomas

## You're the Right Mom For Your Kids

Moms sometimes explode like volcanoes. Moms sometimes hiss like a balloon leaking air. Moms have human feelings and being a mom doesn't take that away. So when you feel big feelings and small feelings, know you're still the right mom for your kids. Take care of yourself. When was the last time you drank water, ate protein, slept well, or moved lovingly? Don't be so hard on yourself. Just do one tiny act of care. Choose to love yourself.

Christy Thomas

I love throwing socks at my kids. It feels like an indoor snowball fight. I find socks months later between a couch and a wall. My kids quickly understand the game and throw socks at me. Whatever was wrong on the day is neutralized by novelty and laughter. Motherhood is serious, but it doesn't have to be serious all the time.

You're the Right Mom For Your Kids

Check In

♡    🖐    🧠
HEART   HAND   MIND

Christy Thomas

Timeouts shouldn't be saved just for kids. Moms can take them, too. Here's an easy one: find a candle and a lighter. Sit down at the kitchen table, light the candle, and watch the flame. Let the flame be your focus and slowly notice your breath. Stay until you hear cries of hunger, danger, or anger. Rest is fuel for your heart—motherhood is a marathon run at a sprint pace. You can rest and the world won't fall apart. Let the flame inspire you to shine brightly with love. You're the right mom.

# You're the Right Mom For Your Kids

Christy Thomas

I'm so glad you're here on Earth. I'm so excited about it. Mathematically, you are impossible. The fact that you are alive is a probability of **1 in $10^{2,685,000}$** — yes, that's a ten followed by 2,685,000 zeroes. So give yourself a hug. It's a good day to have a good enough day. That's all you need.

# You're the Right Mom For Your Kids

There used to be a necklace trend where a girl would get a new pearl to add to a string every birthday. Eventually, she would have a complete pearl necklace, one pearl at a time. Life is like that, too. All the good moments are slowly added, one at a time. The thing is, though, your brain is wired to remember the bad ones. That brain hack has kept humans safe for all these years. So do yourself a favor and start writing down each day what went right because of you. No good moment is too small tonight. Moving the ant out of the way counts. A smile and a nod do, too.

Christy Thomas

I love to wear earrings. "The bigger the hoops, the closer to heaven," is a motto for me. I feel vibrant and fully alive. When my kids were old enough not to pull at them, I started wearing them again. What do you wear that makes you feel like you? Maybe it's lace underwear, nail polish, red lipstick, hair that's dyed expertly. You are a whole human. You're the right mom for your kids and deserve to feel FULLY alive.

# You're the Right Mom For Your Kids

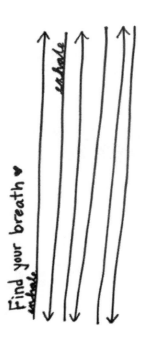

Christy Thomas

There might be something you're comparing yourself to about another mom about that makes you feel less than. I have a secret. She probably has something she's reaching for, too. We don't need to compete with each other. Celebrate with me. I want to cheer loudly for you.

You're the Right Mom For Your Kids

Christy Thomas

Life is confusing, beautiful, fragile, and wonderful. Find your kids, hug them, or text them a meme. Do it right now. Let them know how much you love them. You are just the right mom.

# You're the Right Mom For Your Kids

Hugs are anchored to each other. Find one of your humans and hug them for 20 seconds. Your body will relax and calm. Hugs help us know when we are home. You are home for your kids. Remind them.

## You're the Right Mom For Your Kids

Gentle parenting that doesn't include the mom being human, too, isn't gentle. Don't feel guilt or shame for needing breaks or caring for relationships outside of your kids. Don't feel guilty about exercise or hygiene or choosing meals that feel good to you but your kids hate. You're the right mom for your kids & a human, too.

Christy Thomas

When I feel helpless about the big world, I go small. I focus on my house. Have a family dinner. Tell bad jokes. Go to piano lessons. Hug a lot. Pray and take deep breaths. I remember to have a glass of water and not wine so I can sleep well. Then, I get to bed on time. Tomorrow will be a chance to wake up and love again.

## You're the Right Mom For Your Kids

Are you having a hard time with one specific kid? Find the baby photos and put them where you can't help but see them. I hang them inside the kitchen cabinet with coffee mugs. By the front door. My nightstand. I remind myself that they are humans learning to be humans. Sometimes, I post a picture of myself as a baby as well. I'm a human still learning to be human. You are, too. I'm so glad you're here. You're the right human to be alive right now.

Christy Thomas

When was the last time you stood in the grass with your arms outstretched, face up to the sun? Consider treating yourself like a complicated houseplant. Sun? Water? Fresh air? Those will help you come home to yourself. It's easy to get caught up in the to-do list of raising humans. Be excessively gentle with yourself. You are loved.

## You're the Right Mom For Your Kids

Mom Hack: Add sprinkles to applesauce (I like it warmed) and it's an instant fancy dessert. Sprinkles on cereal, oatmeal, and toast make breakfast better. I've never added sprinkles to steak, but that might work too. Surprise yourself with novelty and joy. You're worth it. You're the right mom for your kids.

Christy Thomas

The next time your kids laugh at a joke or tell you something hilarious— slyly pull out the voice memo app on your phone. Your kids' saved laughter will brighten your future and bad days. The days are long, but the years are short. It's worth documenting the ordinary.

## You're the Right Mom For Your Kids

Stay in the photo— take the selfies with your kids. Take the selfies by yourself. Smile. Laugh. Cry. Capture all of you. Someday, you will look back and see how gorgeous and vibrant you were while raising kids. You are a knockout.

Christy Thomas

I want to be a happy mom laughing at the dining room table more than I want to be a fancy mom with a three-course meal. Some people are talented enough to do both. I'm not. That's okay. I'll choose pre-cut veggies, simple meals, and even paper plates. I choose what will help me enjoy motherhood the most. Let's be the happiest moms we know.

You're the Right Mom For Your Kids

— check in —
fresh air?
water?
sunshine?
Kind words?

Christy Thomas

Raindrops on roses and whiskers on kittens are not a few of my favorite things. Folded laundry put away, freshly combed hair, laughter and giggles, and shoes in a straight line by the door. Those are some of my favorite things. Dances, card games, and walks for flowers are the moments that make up my days. The tiny moments aren't so tiny when you look back at them.

## You're the Right Mom For Your Kids

I'm trying to learn how to knit. I want to create something that I can see progress with. It's funny to my kids that I have a hobby. I must show them that my life is as significant as theirs. My love is obsessed with them, but my life needs to be diverse and vibrant so adulthood looks like joy. I want to take the pressure off my kids– my joy is independent of their happiness. I'm an entire person, even while mothering them. You are, too. Take care of yourself.

Christy Thomas

## Truths

When you pick up the cheerios on the floor- it's holy.

When you hold the baby and wipe the nose- it's holy.

When you rub their back and hum lullabies- it's holy.

When you give long hugs and breathe in the smell of your child- it's holy.

Motherhood is millions of tiny things and your love is holy.

Give yourself a moment to see with your heart, not your to-do list.

It's all holy.

# You're the Right Mom For Your Kids

Christy Thomas

Turn off the scroll. Oh, Mama. You don't need to compare yourself to anyone else. The matching pj's holiday photos are lovely– but nothing compares to holding the sticky hand of a toddler. Motherhood isn't a competition. It's a community of hearts. Let's open ours bigger. You are the right mom for your kids. Racoon eyes, messy clothes, sticky floors, and sticky hands are good.

## MAKER OF MEMORIES— MOM

What memories do you want to pull up when you are 80? Your favorites will most likely be ordinary things on ordinary days. So right now, take the photos with you in them– make the memories. And just so we are on the same page, you do not need to enjoy every moment of motherhood to have good memories of motherhood. Even messes can be beautiful and have silver linings when you look back on them.

Christy Thomas

"I like long sleeves on my legs."

Kids say the best things. Don't fix them. Repeat them–enjoy how much there is to learn as a human. "Ele-gator" will always be better than an elevator.

You're the Right Mom For Your Kids

Christy Thomas

Macaroni and cheese, oatmeal, ramen, yogurt parfait, pancakes, eggs, cheese and crackers, fruit smoothies, brownies, ice cream, popcorn, nuggets, pizza, corn dogs, and cheerios are all main dishes for dinner at my house.

You're the Right Mom For Your Kids

Christy Thomas

Use the paper plates and serve the food. Linger and laugh. Food is what kids need– food and <u>your</u> love.

## You're the Right Mom For Your Kids

Wiping up pee isn't fun— I gave up potty training three times. Sometimes, Mama, we rush our kids. Can we rush a tree into bloom? Nope— breathe that in. We can't rush our kids either. You've got more time than you think. Relax your jaw and breathe.

Christy Thomas

My favorite place to hide with preschoolers is under the comforter in my own bed. Try it– add extra clean laundry on top of the bed if you have school agers. Enjoy the lazy play.

# You're the Right Mom For Your Kids

"Is it poison?" My dear middle child asked me when I gave her the prettiest red apple. That's what I get for reading and watching fairy tales. Feed the imagination and savor the stories. There are real dangers out there– but our kids need joy and creativity more. Feed them stories of dragon slayers in the safety of your lap.

Christy Thomas

When was the last time you bought new underwear? Are your socks holey? Do you eat standing up from the scraps on your kids' plates? Did you wash your face or brush your teeth yesterday? When was the last time you went to a doctor just for you? I need you to love yourself. Even while you mother kids, you get to be a priority, a main character.

## You're the Right Mom For Your Kids

What are your favorite things? Do you even remember? I bet images of your kids' favorites popped up first. That's so amazing– you are so attentive! So loving! So curious! You notice everything about your kids. Notice yourself, too. Wear your favorite color. Wear your favorite lipstick, jewelry, and perfume. Don't wait until your kids are grown to remember what you like– do it now.

Christy Thomas

"Happiness always looks small while you hold it in your hand." Maxim Groky

Mama, it's so easy for your brain to remember the bad parts of the day. When you go to bed tonight, collect the small happy moments. Every single good, small, minuscule crumb of happiness counts.

You're the Right Mom For Your Kids

Christy Thomas

Relax your shoulders, wiggle your toes, shake your hands, and unclench your jaw. Somedays, poop is thrown at you (real and figurative). Expect it. You are your kid's safe place. You are still and always have been exactly the right mom for your kids.

# You're the Right Mom For Your Kids

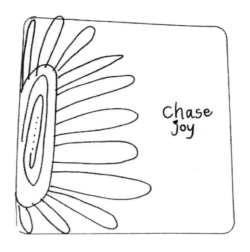

Christy Thomas

Things I never want near my face: Toes. Other people's buggers. Burps. Farts. Vomit.
And even with that list, I'm still a fun mom and a loving mom. No one needs all the access to you.

You're the Right Mom For Your Kids

Christy Thomas

More important than "I love you," say "I'm sorry." Show your kids that even adults make mistakes. No one needs to be perfect to be loved. Teach yourself how to repair and fail a little better next time. Lead with grace.

## You're the Right Mom For Your Kids

Monsters Inc. was right— kids' unbridled laughter can fuel the whole planet. Moms get to be funny – tell the jokes, be silly, pretend to fall with style, pull the safe pranks, sing in falsetto and opera. Don't let dads have all the fun— you get to be unserious too.

Christy Thomas

I don't regret being late if it means I didn't yell. Let that sink in. The world has forgotten the speed of children. Disappoint the right people. Stay connected to your kid above all else.

There is no perfect way to do laundry, fold sheets, or load the dishwasher. There's no "police" for vacuum lines on the carpet. Dust bunnies are still found in Buckingham Palace. Your worth as a mom isn't found in perfect care tasks. The value of motherhood is located in the secure attachment of kids who feel safe with you.

Christy Thomas

If another mom loves slime and you hate it– don't yuck on her yum.
If another mom dresses to the tens when you live in yoga pants– don't yuck on her yum.
If you have a crunchy BFF and you love orange Cheetos and red pop – don't yuck on her yum.
If you work in an office and your buddy stays home– don't yuck on her yum.
If you school differently, it's not a competition– don't yuck on her yum.

We need moms different from us. Our kids need the love that all moms can give. Let's invite everyone in. The more, the merrier in motherhood. You belong.

## You're the Right Mom For Your Kids

I locked my sleeping toddler in the car in my driveway. All the spare keys were in the car with him. It was a hot spring day with full sun. I called 911 and asked for help. I stood next to him the whole time. That sweet, sweaty hug was the best hug ever.*

*Good moms make mistakes, hug yourself for me.

Christy Thomas

Most motherhood isn't an emergency. Slow down and wait for the real one. It will come, you'll be ok, and practicing for it won't help. Instead, take the longest exhale (like blowing out candles) and count to 5 with the next inhale. Exhale, Inhale. Life is unexpected with kids. But you don't need to add extra panic.

Things I've called poison control for

- Sidewalk chalk
- Cat food
- Body wash (Irish Spring)
- Benadryl
- Mint toothpaste
- Jr. Tylenol

Some of those things were really, really scary, **BUT** mistakes happen. Poison control has the friendliest nurses ever. I'm still a good mom, even in the scariest of moments when I call for help. You are, too.

Christy Thomas

I locked my kids inside my house while they were sleeping—stupid trashcans. I threw rocks at the windows, and they wouldn't wake up. It was 10 PM– my husband was deployed. I called a friend who brought me a sweatshirt and waited for the locksmith. Sometimes, you'll be the one who needs help. Other times, you'll be the friend who helps. Motherhood is too fragile to do alone– make many friends and many copies of your house key.

## You're the Right Mom For Your Kids

Sometimes, something IS wrong with our kids. My kiddo is behind 95% of her peers with speech. I had no clue. I understood her just fine. This is still not a panic moment, it's a team-building moment. Motherhood isn't a solo sport. Find teachers, doctors, therapists, friends, librarians, and family who can help you. It's a crisis, but you'll get through it with a team. Love your perfect and unique kids just as they are right now. Advocate for them, hold all of their hopes and dreams.

## Christy Thomas

These clothing choices are all appropriate for a child in the grocery store.

- superhero
- Princess
- Firefighter
- Winter coat in summer
- Shorts in winter
- Outfit of 1000000000 layers
- Ensemble of too many colors
- Mismatched shoes
- Frog boots, even when there is a drought
- PJs
- Fancy clothes
- Muddy clothes
- Bathrobe
- CLOTHES

If a stranger or cashier makes a snide comment, just shrug and say– "At least the most essential things are covered." You are totally winning in my book. Take a selfie with your kid. You're going to really, really want this photo when they are sixteen. I promise.

Dear Mama, did you wake up crying in the middle of the night? Maybe hunger, sickness, or bad dreams. The needs of others often break up your sleep. You won't always be tired, so go easy on yourself. Take a nap when they nap. I go to bed early sometimes. Ask for help. <3

Christy Thomas

Do you hate slime? What about playdough? I'm not too fond of store-bought stuff in bright yellow cans, but I delight in making it on the stove. Kneading it is relaxing. I like to add in essential oils. Play can also be a delight for you if you let it be. Pro Tip: Grab cookie sheets for your kids to work with playdough on if the mess drives you mad.

Here's my mom's playdough recipe:

2 cups flour

2 cups water

1 cup salt

2 tablespoons oil

4 teaspoons cream of tartar

*Food coloring or essential oil optional

Combine ingredients in a saucepan. Cook over low heat for 5-10 minutes. When thickened, remove from the heat. *Add dye or essential oil. Let sit for 2 minutes, and then knead on the counter. Store in an airtight container.

Here's my gluten-free one:
1 cup baby rice cereal
1 cup cornstarch
½ cup applesauce
3 tablespoons of oil
*food coloring

In a medium bowl, mix together rice cereal and cornstarch. Add applesauce and oil. Add optional food color when combined well and knead by hand until well blended. Store in an airtight container.

I love my minivan. It's where I could legally restrain my children and have a physical break from all the touching. I'd say "Let's drive," then pop on an audiobook or kids' music and go. The Starbucks drive-through knew my order – caramel macchiato and two small cups of water with straws.

I'd drive and unwind. I'd drive and laugh. I'd drive and count flags. I'd go and talk about stories and memories. I'd drive and reset my touched-out state and be ready again. If you need a break and can't find someone to help, try your car. Be safe together.

Christy Thomas

Smile at yourself in the mirror. I used to rush by without looking at myself, just knowing that I was lookin' a hot mess. But then, I wondered what would happen if I smiled at myself once a day. I used it as a moment to say motherhood is exhausting AND wonderful, AND it's okay to feel both. You've survived 100% of your worst days so far. Smile at yourself even when you can't smile at life. <3

## You're the Right Mom For Your Kids

How many languages do you know? Did you only think of Spanish, French, German, and Chinese? Sign language or Pig Latin? You know more. You see the body language of an infant who can't talk. You know the grunts of a pre-talker. You interpret the babble of a new talker who doesn't have many sounds. You know the language of why, why, why of a preschooler. You know the language of YOUR child, each of your children. You are an expert, connected by love and 10,000 hours. Give yourself credit for knowing.

Christy Thomas

It's hard to yell if you're blowing bubbles. Remember that. You might need it when you are on your last thread of adulting. Don't just let our kids do it– blow bubbles, too. This works well even in the winter. Just bring the bubbles into the bathtub or shower.

## You're the Right Mom For Your Kids

I have been blessed by children who are climbers. At some point, they may be more billy goats than humans. My chairs live on top of the table like the end of a school day. My chairs have been removed entirely from the room. Moms are creative geniuses when they need to keep young people from dancing at the table at all hours. If you have ever lived in this specific chaos– you're doing a good enough job of motherhood. Decorating trends can wait.

Christy Thomas

I spilled a gallon of milk inside my month-old brand new minivan. We lived in California. I had a toddler and an infant and tried to carry too much. I promise– asking for help is better than hours of wet, dry vac, nature enzyme, and still smelling it 12 years later. And yes, if you spill milk in your car, you have every right to cry. I sure did.

There's been a sleeping bag under my bed for 13 years. We moved it there when my preschooler couldn't sleep all night alone. She could walk to our room and snuggle up in it. She sleeps alone now, but the sleeping bag is there. Just in case. (It happened gradually, and I miss it.) There is no sleep police– do what works for BOTH of you. When that stops working, you get to try something new. Being gentle with both of you.

Christy Thomas

Here is the list of preschool/cartoon theme songs I know of:
Dora, Wonderpets, Umizoomi, Bubble Guppies, Paw Patrol, Give A Mouse A Cookie, Curious George, Sesame Street, Arthur, Daniel Tiger, Super Why, Tumble Leaf, and Odd Squad.

I don't enjoy TV, I don't. But my kids did. Do you know random facts because of your kids? Guess what? That's love in action.

## You're the Right Mom For Your Kids

Maybe you thought you'd only have wooden toys and play silks? And your kid loves loves loves a noisy purple battery-powered plastic computer and a red fire truck. Let it go— release the dream. Love the kid and the moment you have. If you still want wood toys— buy them for decoration and play with them yourself.

## Christy Thomas

I don't sort my laundry. I don't fold my sheets. I don't match my socks. These things might drive you crazy, but they keep my stress level low so I can live each day, not just get through it with frazzled nerves. As I get older, I want to show my kids how to enjoy life more. I want joy more than I want unwrinkled sheets or shirts.

## You're the Right Mom For Your Kids

I tried color-coded schedules and I failed. I tried strict preschool-at-home plans and I failed. I tried rotating grains for snacks and I failed. I tried teaching my baby to read and I failed. I failed. I failed. I failed.

I fail a lot in life when I forget my personal truths. I'm a go-with-the-flow, flexible, and "embrace a little bit of chaos" person.

You do you. That's how you'll be exactly the right, good enough mom for your kids.

Christy Thomas

You know how when you play cards there are rules? I have house rules, too. House rules say I must always kiss my husband goodbye. House rules say we try to Rickroll each other as often as possible. House rules say the best lullaby of all time is the Silly Lullaby by Sandra Boynton. House rules say if you hug mom, she lets go last. I only have three house rules that I had my kids memorize– safety, kindness, and fun with the motto: "I've always liked you just the way you are."

## You're the Right Mom For Your Kids

There was a season in my home when every single room in my house had a basket of toys in it: laundry room, bathroom, kitchen, and foyer. My kids needed my eyes on them to stay alive, and I needed to get things done. So I made space for them. Fight for your kids and the need for ease. Fight for it, not against it. You'll find it, even if it's different than you planned.

Christy Thomas

## You're the Right Mom For Your Kids

Sometimes, I sit on my kids- pretending they aren't there. It's a game called Lumpy Couch. I complain about how strange this "couch" is and how we desperately need a new couch or chair. Really, I'm just glad that they are home. My heart explodes when I realize that I am still as close to my kids now as when they were small. You can have that, too.

Christy Thomas

Secret handshakes are one of my favorite things. I've had so many over the years with my kids. They range from simple to so crazily complex they feel like a dance contest. If you're lonely for your kids at goodbyes and hellos, add a secret handshake ritual. It's good for both of you.

## You're the Right Mom For Your Kids

I painted a guest bedroom in someone else's house because my kids drew on the walls. I ate dinner with other adults in a different room and obviously, in hindsight, made the wrong choice. I have never been a perfect mom since my children arrived. If you ever need a fist bump and a pep talk, imagine a crayon-drawn mural by six kids on renters' white walls. Life happens, and when it does, I'll scrub and repaint with you.

Christy Thomas

I like to cry in the shower. My aunt taught my mom, and my mom taught me. I cry all the tears and wash my hair. I watch it all go down the drain. When you need to press pause- know at least two other moms are crying at that exact moment, too. You might feel alone, but you aren't. You are precisely the right, good enough mom for your kids. Feel the feelings with honesty. You don't need to hide them, but a shower for me is the best place to let them go.

## You're the Right Mom For Your Kids

I am an inconsistent parent. I wobble and change my mind. I make rules and don't stick to them. We have routines. We have rhythms. We have traditions. We have the love that anchors. But just as I'd want a police officer to listen to me if I get pulled over for driving too fast on the way to the Emergency Room, I pause and offer that grace to my kids when they need it. No rule is worth tyranny. I choose growth and humanity.

Christy Thomas

# You're the Right Mom For Your Kids

Ten hugs a day, ten hugs a day– remember what the doctors say, ten hugs a day (I'm singing this). If you're reading this with three or more hours left until bedtime, make it your goal to get ten hugs for you and each child in your house.

Christy Thomas

Hot take– gentle parenting that doesn't include the mom being human isn't gentle. Don't guilt or shame yourself for needing breaks. For taking care of relationships outside of your kids. For exercise, hygiene, or meals that feel good to you but your kids hate. You are the right mom for your kids & YOU are a wonderful, fantastic human being.

## You're the Right Mom For Your Kids

I could listen to the negative voice in my head because it's always there, but I choose the compassionate one instead. Ending the day with fun, playing a quick game before bed, cuddling, and dancing. I could choose to think I failed today. Instead, let's both choose to cap each day with connection and joy.

Christy Thomas

It's not a mistake that you have the kids you do. You're exactly the right mom for them. Take a deep breath and say a quick prayer. Drink some water. Trust me. You're the right mom for your kids. I'm cheering you on forever and always.

## You're the Right Mom For Your Kids

Some people love spotless counters or fresh vacuum lines. I instantly love my house more when I clean my windows. Know yourself. I'm a better mom when the golden sunlight streams in. I'm more present, more calm, and more loving What settles your soul? Do more of that so you can love from the overflow.

Christy Thomas

## You're the Right Mom For Your Kids

No one else is responsible for your joy. It's your job to manage it, refill it, rest in it, rediscover it, and bring it with you. Do you have a plan for refilling your joy during the day? Or do you drag yourself through and countdown until bedtime? Your heart and your body know— listen to her. You have a beacon of joy in you.

Christy Thomas

If you want to keep your memories, you must live them first. You make the memories in ordinary moments. You make the memories in the dark moments. You make memories in the sad moments. You make memories in extraordinary moments. You make the memories when you live in the moment.

## You're the Right Mom For Your Kids

My favorite place to play games is at my dining room table. I love to make centerpieces of games in the middle of it. Why let them grow dusty in my closet? I decorate for the kids that live here. Flowers and candles sometimes, but always decks of cards and games.

Christy Thomas

## You're the Right Mom For Your Kids

On the dark nights of the soul (and life in general), it is easy to get wrapped up in a blanket of doubt. While life can be complex and full of suffering, you've never been the wrong mom for your kids. There are no spare parts in humanity's mosaic. Hold on to hope. Look for the tiny cracks of light and laughter around you. I'm so glad you and your child are here. You are exactly the right mom for this moment and your child. You are loved, and the darkness will fade, I promise.

Christy Thomas

When you are scared in motherhood waiting for the diagnosis, a shoe to drop, a label for your child, you are doing holy work.
When you lament,
"Why God?"
You are doing holy work.
When you make grilled cheese cut on the diagonal as comfort food for a sick child, you are doing holy work.
When you share your pain with your community and ask for support, you are doing holy work.
When motherhood feels raw and leaves your heart fully naked, you are doing holy work.

I need to be honest with you— well, more open with you. Grief is always part of motherhood. Grief over developmental challenges. Grief over the unexpected. Grief over broken hearts and loss. When I became a mom, I didn't expect the constant cycle of loving so much my heart could burst and mourning the loss of the phases my kids were in. No one told me that part. You never know the last time you rocked a baby to sleep until months later. So be excessively gentle and kind to yourself if your heart holds more grief than you can label. Don't rush feelings away. Sit with it and breathe. The seasons are constantly changing, and a bloom of hope is already budding.

Christy Thomas

When the going gets tough, do less and be more. Be more present. Be closer. Be still and notice. Be the anchor of love. Ruthlessly remove all the fluff– Say no to requests that don't provide food, water, shelter, or soul care for your family. Breathe slowly– Notice your exhale and let your body soften. Just be.

## You're the Right Mom For Your Kids

My kids HATE goodbyes. At playdates early in their lives, they often asked to borrow toys from their friends' homes. They knew we had to see the people again to return them.

They hate goodbyes for people, goodbyes for places, goodbyes for pets. I've learned not to rush this with my children. It works to sit beside them—offering comfort with hugs, back rubs, and physical closeness. Feelings like this are why we can love so big. Don't shame them out. Sitting with your kids' feelings might be tricky if no one sits with yours. Sitting with them isn't wrong or too soft. You are loving. You are safe. You are loved. Don't try to fix goodbyes and heartaches. Just be near.

Christy Thomas

Kids meltdown for those they feel safe with. Kids meltdown for those who listen well. Kids meltdown for those they can trust. Meltdowns are code for enormous, overwhelming feelings– anger, sadness, joy, excitement, love, fear, nervousness, grief. Kids trusting us with their feelings is a sacred privilege– we hold their hearts gently with open, soft hands and hearts.

## Christy Thomas

My last living grandparents died back to back to back in 2021 and 2022. My heart and body couldn't keep up with grief. I noticed sadness lingering until I started sharing memories. It's right to protect kids from the horrors of the world – but we can't protect them from the pain of love. Learn from me. Try not to withdraw because of the pain and confuse your kids into thinking they are the problem. Instead, find ways to celebrate the memories and goodness of being alive.

## You're the Right Mom For Your Kids

Don't give up on motherhood. Don't be surprised when life changes and brings you doubt. Not knowing grief and pain are part of motherhood is not planted in reality. If you're lucky enough to hug your children before bed tonight, do it again for a mom who can't.

Christy Thomas

I hope our kids grow up to notice the clouds. or

Today, I saw light streaming through the clouds at sunset. "Look! Look!" Don't miss it!" I urged my kids as we drove across town. The light looked majestic and perfect on the fluffy white and gray clouds. From a different angle, those clouds could look heavy with rain and storms as minutes later, they poured. Perspective always matters– there are storms in motherhood. I can't stop them. You can't stop them. Be ready to spot the light and the storm. Breathe in the gift of both.

## Christy Thomas

At the science museum today, I learned about the light pollution scale. It helps you predict the number of stars you'll be able to see at night. In the darkest spots, you can observe the Milky Way; in the brightest areas, you can see only one or two stars in the sky. In my life, "Light Pollution" is the endless scroll of social media. My eyes become so vast from the brightness of others that my view of my true self is almost gone. Find the quiet and dark moments to know you are the right mom for your kids. You are a good mom– a good enough mom. Your love changes everything; don't pollute it, turn off the lights, and rest.

## You're the Right Mom For Your Kids

Sometimes, mothers can't cure sickness, grumpiness, depression, grief, or pain. All you can do is be with your child. Be the love. Be the back rub. Be the joke and the smile. Be the cup of water in the middle of the night. Be available for the meme, the text, and the whisper. Don't give up on your kid– it's your fantastic opportunity to love them even when they don't act like they want love. They do. They are afraid to say they need more. You can be afraid to ask, too. Love and BE anyway.

Christy Thomas

When you need help, don't silence yourself. Don't wish your partner, family, or kids could read your mind. Ask. Ask. Ask. Use that shaky voice. And then when someone says– Yes, I'll do it., say "thank you" and let them do it however it looks. Let them love you– you are so loveable. Limitations and imperfections. All of you is loved.

Christy Thomas

Moving is a hard, hard, hard thing. I've moved cross-country – 1, 2, 3, 4, 5, 6, 7,8, 9, 10 times. It's not just sorting, packing, and unpacking. But the packing and unpacking of who you are. You can now try new things, you can stay the same, you can meet new friends, you can keep the old ones. You can be off-kilter. You can be full of excitement and bliss. It's okay– just know you can grow roots wherever you are. You can bloom where you are planted new. Give yourself 12 months to learn the new place. Roots take time.

## You're the Right Mom For Your Kids

Motherhood can feel so heavy, from the unseen tasks that only have value when you have to pay someone else to do it or when the ball gets dropped. Scratch that— actually, the care tasks don't belong to motherhood. We've been tricked. Care tasks are just part of adulthood. Motherhood is your heart outside your body, bursting with love and dreams. Motherhood success isn't measured by completed laundry.

Christy Thomas

How do you whisper to another mom that you need help? Do you need emotional support? You bravely look at her shoes and then in her eyes and whisper that motherhood is tricky (because it is), Or you send a text that says, "I want to quit " That other mom knows– if she responds with a safe, soft spot of "me too" and where would you go, you've got a village. Text back a hug and a GIF, and plan an imaginary vacation. Hold on to her– that's your village. One honest moment at a time– and I promise, now, when she has a hard day, she'll text you, too.

Things that I love when I am grieving

- Face masks
- Ginger tea
- Cozy socks
- Fuzzy blankets, no matter the season
- Warm showers
- 90s boy bands and Harry Styles
- My rosary
- Crayons and coloring books
- Long hugs
- Green Smoothies
- Crunchy snacks
- Cuddles

Christy Thomas

Things I remember to do when I am grieving

- None of those things

Note to self: On a happy day – write down a list of cozy things. Save it on your phone and use it as a menu to pick from. Be excessively gentle with yourself, dear heart. You are the right human to feel feelings. You are the right human to be alive. You are the best mom.

# You're the Right Mom For Your Kids

Fill me in with color + doodles. ♥ct

## Christy Thomas

My teenager is super stressed out. She's not her usual talkative self to me, and her face has a mild frown. I know there's no magic wand for the complex, emotional teen years. But I decided to wash her feet. I gathered a towel, a hot foot bath, peppermint lotion, and nail polish and invited her. In the end, I rubbed lotion into her legs, which are sturdy and strong and brave. I rubbed her piggy toes and kept the nursery rhyme to myself. I saw a glimmer of peace and nourishment in her eyes. It was all worth it. Do the extra thing. Humble yourself with love.

Inhale and exhale. Unclench your jaw. Relax your shoulders. Wiggle your fingers, elbows, wrists, and toes. Jump up and down. Inhale and exhale again, this time picturing the breath coming in through your heart, spreading love all around your body with each heartbeat. Exhale through your heart all stress and fear. All will be well. All is well. Miracles are all around you.

Christy Thomas

## You're the Right Mom For Your Kids

Moments are what make a life. In some cases, the moments are cleaning up vomit, wiping tears, rubbing backs, watching fevers and rashes, endless feedings, and changing diapers. Sometimes, the moment is awe– watching siblings meet for the first time, first words, first steps, first favorites, first concerts, first time reading, biking, skating, rolling, sports, concerts, sacraments at church. Sometimes, in mothering, I want the moment to speed ahead like a bullet train. There are others where I want to freeze it and travel back to be amazed over and over and over again. When you meet another mom, you don't know where in that range she is. So be excessively kind. In the best and worst, we need the village of other mothers. Remind her that she's exactly the right mom for her kids. Remember to linger and hug your kids today. Let go last and text those who aren't close enough to hug.

## Christy Thomas

For many, there's a moment in motherhood when you realize that your kids have gotten bigger than you. Bigger hands. Bigger feet. Bigger bottomless stomachs. Taller. Stronger. Do you remember when you grew bigger than your parents? How odd that feeling is. Don't forget the importance of hugging your children's big bodies. You can scuff their hair with your hands and squeeze their shoulders. Don't let their physical size make you scared to share your heart.

## You're the Right Mom For Your Kids

I watched a mom at the grocery store as her preschooler talked very, very loudly about grapes, apples, and oranges. Others noticed as well and shot eyes that said, "Shush, that's not an inside voice." As a society, we've forgotten how delightful and joyful children can be. Finding the perfect yellow and red apple, big squishy grapes, and oranges with belly buttons is a delight. I waved and whispered a prayer. May they be safe, may they be well, may they be loved. I whisper prayers and blessings whenever I see a mom and child out and about. Motherhood is too important and too fragile to do alone.

Christy Thomas

## You're the Right Mom For Your Kids

What do you do when the baby no longer fits the baby clothes? The crib? The car seat? The stroller? It would be best if you let yourself feel all the feelings. Joy and delight are okay. Grief and dismay are okay, too. Apprehension and excitement are also welcome. I want you to know that motherhood is constantly changing. We learn how to adapt to these changes, little by little. You'll find they're never too big for hugs.

Christy Thomas

Moms are often lonely– they turn to social media for connection. That's okay and valid, and it makes sense. You can be inspired. You can be comforted. You can offer comfort. You can share tips and tricks. Just know you can always turn it off. We don't need you to perform for us and miss your own life. I love Instagram, but I don't live there, and you don't either. It's important to me that I keep my feet planted and nourish my real life every day.

# You're the Right Mom For Your Kids

When was the last time you planned a sabbatical? Have you let your kids see you rest? I'm in a moment of burnout and feel like I can't relax. It's the complete opposite of the truth. I need to rest. I show up as the human I want to be when I feel love overflowing. When I'm too tired and think I can't take a break, I break out this list.

– I read a poem
– I dance
– I stretch
– I place my hand on my heart & breathe
– I rest with my legs resting against a wall over me
– I empty the sink and run the dishwasher
– I vacuum
– I set a timer and play a game on my phone

Christy Thomas

How can we make motherhood easier? Can we choose to look for simple ways to love and not guilt ourselves about it? Can you permit yourself not to make motherhood hard? Motherhood is serious and dedicated work– but it's not a job of martyrdom. It's an art of love.

# You're the Right Mom For Your Kids

My son is afraid of the basement, but only at bedtime. It's taken many, many moments of patience to figure all of this out. When you slow down and listen fully to all the little things, you invest in your relationship with your kids. That way, when the big stuff comes— vulnerability, mistakes, fears, loneliness- you are a trusted and safe spot. Hold your kids' words gently, treat them like precious jewels, and cherish your bond.

Christy Thomas

## A poem for my child

Take my finger
Hold it
With your brand new body
Eyes closed, so sweet
I'm the lucky one


Take my hand
Hold it
You're chubby, wobbly legs
Barely standing
I'm the lucky one


Take my heart
Hold it
With your soft, perfect heart
Always connected
No matter the miles
I'm the lucky one

## You're the Right Mom For Your Kids

Keep your wild dreams and a wild heart. Teach your sons and daughters the most significant way to love is by first loving and valuing the miracle of yourself.

Christy Thomas

We live far away from family. Sometimes, that means our family connections feel shaky. During a recent visit, I snuggled in my sheets, scrolling websites, looking for a perfect puzzle. Grandparents were visiting, and I didn't know how to start the conversation. One thousand pieces from a Swedish fishing village brought everyone to the table. We sat and sorted. Conversations wandered and woven. We had to eat our meals on the couch for a few days. There was a race for the last puzzle piece. It's a moment I'll forever cherish.

## You're the Right Mom For Your Kids

Tonight, I was my daughter's date to a high school band concert. It was a pure delight: small smiles, whispers, hand squeezing. Time slipped fast through her school career. I'll say "yes" to every moment I possibly can.

Christy Thomas

I know a mama of one who is praying for more. My hands and heart are open and soft, waiting with her. Are you a mama waiting, too? You're not alone. If you're ever feeling wobbly, you can lean on the rest of us.

## You're the Right Mom For Your Kids

A typhoon hit an island in the middle of the Pacific with people I love on it. Before the storm, I texted, asking how a mom was doing. I wondered how they filled the hours trapped inside by dangerous wind. She apologized and said "Too much screen time." If I could, I'd lift her chin and say, "You're making great choices for your kids with what you have. Keep doing that."

Christy Thomas

Not all of us will face a typhoon with three kids alone on an island. But you are doing the best you can in this crazy moment. No judgment– I assume you always make the best choice out of the crappy ones. You are loved. You are loved.

When you feel stressed, your body first responds to a physical threat– even if it's email or kid noise. These three questions can help you filter out the danger:

1. How serious is this really?
2. What is essential here?
3. How can I make it easier?

Are you holding on to a spill or mess? Holding a grudge? Pause and ask. What have I hired the grudge to do? What emotion is it really covering? Wiggle your body and be open to all feelings. Let yourself fire the resentment. Move towards love.

Toxic positivity isn't helpful in mothering. Shine a spotlight on it. Ask "What's missing?" instead of "What's wrong?" What's missing shows you that something is changeable. When you have the most options, you feel the most free. You'll find motherhood is limitless.

Christy Thomas

We played a new game last night after dinner. "Egyptian War" is a card game similar to Solitaire but played in a group. It starts slow and feels random and lively. We played it because I planned it– I googled it. I printed it. I learned it. I made it happen. This is my favorite part of motherhood– planning delights and fun.

# You're the Right Mom For Your Kids

> Hey,
> the days are long
> but the 940 weeks
> are short.
> You've got this.

Christy Thomas

Isn't it wonderful to clear the table after dinner? You have a family eating together. You have a table in a house. You have food. You have running water to wash with. Isn't it all wonderful? It's okay not to want to do it, but it is wonderful.

# You're the Right Mom For Your Kids

Try for 12 Hugs a Day

I love cuddling my middle child at bedtime. I used to lie down and fall right asleep next to her. Now, I set a timer because two adult bodies don't fit in a twin bed well. But, the nights I don't get to hear all of her worries and adventures, I miss it.

Christy Thomas

I'm a million different moms today. Soft mom. Grumpy mom. Silly mom. Loud Mom. Attentive Mom. Cuddly Mom. Consistent mom. Fun mom. Standoffish mom. If you've been a million moms today– embrace the chaos. Then act from love. You've always been exactly the right mom.

## You're the Right Mom For Your Kids

Sometimes, kids act like a know-it-alls. They can be intense and full of amazing obscure facts about Roblox, turtles, volcanos, or musicals. Let them teach you. Lean in and be fully enraptured by these fantastic humans. Kids who tell you obscure facts are talking to you. You're doing something right. XOXO

Christy Thomas

I have zero friends who have known all my kids since their births. I have one friend who comes close- we've been nomads together. At a school concert recently, I had a huge wave of jealousy when I observed people who have known each other since their kids started kindergarten. I hired that jealousy to teach me to value what I have. It taught me to value building friendships no matter where I live and how long I live there. I called my person and left a rambling, gushing voicemail– you should call yours, too. <3

## You're the Right Mom For Your Kids

When you're bored in motherhood, add novelty. Tonight, I packed up a bag, a cooler, and three quilts for a picnic. We walked to the car with tons of bluster (no one wanted to leave home). It was simply my five people, a blanket, picnic dinner with live music. We lived it together and it was just fine. It's important to remember you can choose what you like and sometimes bring your kids along too.

## Christy Thomas

Do you have siblings? My brother is 40. I'm 41. I love watching him be a dad. I love being an aunt. Just like my heart is out of my body and walking in my kids, my heart is in my nephew, too. We've lived far away from each other since I married, but the first half of my life is full of him: his laughter, likes, dislikes, TV shows, and hobbies. I'm a better human being because of him. Treasure the bonds you had before becoming a mom. They matter.

# You're the Right Mom For Your Kids

Sometimes, I think I have a memory problem. The memories I most want to hold forever, can't be entirely recalled—laughter, smells of old houses, cuddling and rubbing backs, first cuddles, first love. But I can easily remember the parts that broke my heart. One night, my sweet child remembered one of those unfortunate moments, too. Together, we cracked open our hearts so I could hold them, stay close, and heal.

Christy Thomas

You are exactly the right human to read this. You are not an accidental clump of cells. You are a wonderful creation (and yes, I know 100% that you aren't perfect). You are a vessel of pure love. You are the right mother for your children–exactly the right one.

## You're the Right Mom For Your Kids

I am so honored to love other peoples' kids who live near us. I always want to be the mom who welcomes all the kids and loves them just as they are. We talk about sports, books, movies, music, birds, trees, and video games. My kids are blessed by their friends' moms, too. They've offered comfort and saved the day. They've celebrated my kids without abandon. I'm so thankful for this village. If you have one, value it. If you don't have one, I'll be yours.

## Christy Thomas

My kids each have a favorite sandwich. Ham and Cheese, Tomato and Mozzarella, PB & Jelly. They each have a "cut style." Sometimes, I don't want to take the extra 2 seconds to slice the sandwich just right. But then, I do it, see the twinkle in their eyes, and know it's worth it. Motherhood is full of tiny love notes– this is one of them. It counts because I know they'll remember this. I can't wait to see how they cut sandwiches for their kids. We have things to look forward to.

## You're the Right Mom For Your Kids

I had a running streak. I ran a mile every single day. My kids will remember this. I ran downstairs. I ran around the playground. I ran circles around our house. I ran to the stop sign and back– over and over. I ran, pushing a stroller and with kids biking near me. I ran to love my motherhood body. I ran to love my body into companionship instead of dread. I ran to rewrite the family history of women wanting to change. Your body is your friend.

Christy Thomas

Oreos or some form of cookies go into lunchboxes every school day. There's no shame in store-bought. Want to know what else goes in– a joke? Laughter, bad jokes, and sugar are school-day stress relievers.

Want a joke? Here are a few:

What do you call a snail on a ship? A snail-or!
What do you call an angry vegetable? A steamed carrot.
Why do cows wear bells? Because their horns don't work.
What do sea monsters eat? Fish and ships
What's brown and sticky? A stick.
What do you call a pig who practices karate? A pork chop!
What did the cake say to the fork? You wanna piece of me?!

## You're the Right Mom For Your Kids

You are already the right mom for your kids. You stumble because there are cracks in the sidewalk of life– not because you're not enough.

Christy Thomas

I killed a houseplant after three months. It was my Valentine's Day present. But I have three thriving plants left in my home. Two of them are called prayer-plants. The leaves move down at sunrise and close up like prayer hands at sunset. I whisper to them sweet nothings– if you don't know how to give yourself compliments, get a plant and speak to it.

Compliments can be built this way:
1. My + Noun + is/looks + positive Adjective
    a. *My smile is gorgeous.*
    b. *My laughter bubbles with life.*

2. I + like/love + Noun Phrase.
    a. *I love my creativity.*
    b. *I like my soft curves.*

## You're the Right Mom For Your Kids

Rest is not so that you can prevent brokenness or promote healing. Rest and play are vital to your brain and your heart. Do you nap? Do you have hobbies? What did you love to do at age 5, 10, 15, 20? Can you try those things again? A playful mom is a GIFT to yourself and your family. Your type of play, whatever it is, is precisely what your kids need to see an adult do.

Christy Thomas

We went for a walk to a neighborhood pond after dinner. Family walks are one of my favorite things and don't happen nearly enough. When we got to the dock this evening, my youngest kid yelled STOP! They had noticed tiny jumping baby frogs. HUNDREDS of them. These frogs were as tiny as my thumbnail. We stood, and we watched in awe. Kids give us the gift of being– being fully in the moment. Please show them your moments of AWE and stop for theirs.

# You're the Right Mom For Your Kids

*Check In*

♡ HEART  ✋ HAND  🧠 MIND

I have my first case of poison ivy. I didn't want it. I tried to lather it in homemade potions and lotions. Nothing at all helped the FIRE itchiness until I asked for help. I went to the doctor through an app on my phone while on vacation. As soon as the medicine kicked in, I noticed not only was I not itchy, but I was also kind. I was softer. I was more patient. My whole body was relaxed. You are worth feeling good. You might be surprised by how many things get more manageable when you are honest with yourself and get cared for. You deserve care.

Christy Thomas

"Never less than x, never more than y." Don't panic. I'm not teaching you math. It's just a statement of limits. I found that when I wanted to dabble in a hobby, that is what I needed to be brave enough to start. I could never read less than 3 pages of a fun book daily and never more than 50. I could never doodle for less than 5 minutes daily and never more than 12. I could never meditate for less than 1 minute a day, never more than 10. Limits can be lovely and kind– they help you trust yourself. What can you test out to add joy to your life?

Yelling feels bad for everyone. While yelling, it might feel like a release, but immediatcly after, it doesn't feel very good. If you need to go yell, go yell at a tree, a toilet, or a pillow. If you've yelled, own it. Apologize and let trust build itself back by not yelling. You get to feel safe about yourself, and then your kids get to feel safe, too. You get to make choices that FEEL good, not just the ones that adults did to you. You are healing.

Let go to grow.

Christy Thomas

If parenting has you pulling weeds you didn't know were planted – welcome to the club. I've found the unwanted ideas, patterns, racism, fears, and control growing in my life. Most of these things I unknowingly absorbed from the adults around me as a child, media, books, teachers, family. If you are making a choice NOT to do these things. I am proud of you. You are a heroic cycle breaker and exactly the right mom to make this change. You are exactly the right mom for your kids.

## You're the Right Mom For Your Kids

I recently decided to stop a goal that felt like it was a large part of my personal identity. It took me weeks to whisper that I wanted it to change, and then I decided to share that I wanted a change with my friends. No one told me I was an idiot. No one said to me that I was silly for quitting or changing. One asked if I needed encouragement to keep going or if I was really sure I wanted this change. I thought that was such a sweet question. It allowed me to check in again with myself and say yes– this is what I want.

Christy Thomas

Let's normalize changing things that aren't working on purpose. You don't have to be stuck. How does this apply to motherhood? You don't have to wait until the emergency to dream a different dream. You can make a small change-from how you interact with your kids to your daily schedule. You are free.

# You're the Right Mom For Your Kids

Setting goals allows you to practice being who you want to be– it's about the journey. But when you change the goal after trying it out for a while, you still have learned and grown. That can't be lost. Your identity isn't in the goal or the accomplishment. Your identity is in the legacy of love in the ripples around you.

## Christy Thomas

It's come to my attention that I don't always accept help well. So, not only is it hard to ask for help, but when someone else offers help– I've learned to say no. What a crazy loop! Do you notice this pattern in yourself? I have to remind myself that I'm not a superhero. I know it's obvious, but it's almost essential to say daily. The marketing of moms is that YOU can do it all, can do it well, and aren't replaceable. I've said some of those things to you, even on accident. You aren't replaceable, but you can't do it all simultaneously, and you can't do it well alone. If your child asks to fold towels, let them. If your spouse says he'll drive for the night, don't talk him out. If your friend wants to drop off dinner, say thank you. Our interdependence is a superpower– we are meant to do life together. Let's model that for our kids– it can cure so many problems with the epidemic of loneliness. Say yes to people.

## You're the Right Mom For Your Kids

Close your eyes – okay, don't do it yet. Wait until you read the whole thing, and then close your eyes. I want you to imagine your perfect fantasy morning routine. When does it start? Who is in it? Are you in the countryside of France with roosters and fresh baguettes? Does it involve a rainy day, tea by the window, and eggs benedict? Or a mountainside sunrise hike with a chorus of birds? Close your eyes and feel it all. What is one tiny way you can bring that feeling into your house? Maybe it's your breakfast choice. Perhaps it's a candle or a piece of music in the background. Let's start your day with imagination and hope. You are such a bright light to the world. Don't dim it the moment you wake up– find ways to savor the dreams you have from the moment you get out of bed.

## Christy Thomas

My friend sews butterfly patches all over her overalls. In fact, she wears only overalls with sports bras if she's at home because that's what feels good. She's glowing up by noticing her sensory needs and the need for ease. She loves gardening and caring for her chickens and ducks. A few years ago, this friend was trapped in an urban apartment in Japan with her family. It was not right for her and hard. Soul crushing. But she kept remembering who she was. She's a radical woman and mother who loves with abandon. She took herself on walks. She did puzzles. She listened to audiobooks furiously. If you're like my friend was and trapped in the wrong spot for you, feed your soul now. Text a friend to remind yourself of all of your best traits and live into one of those. Don't give up too soon. We're so glad you're here on Earth with us.

# You're the Right Mom For Your Kids

I celebrate progress. Awareness, not perfection, is the goal. I celebrate connection, not just obedience. Trust and care, not fear, are the goals. Lifelong relationships with imperfect, happy humans is what I want over shiny kids that make me look good. I celebrate the progress found in me and for all the generations before me. Your simple changes change your family tree.

Christy Thomas

Over and over and over again, in the challenging moments, I have to remind myself that I want to be the person my kids turn to when something rough/shaming happens, not who they turn and hide from. I want to prove every day that I am a trustworthy, safe place that loved them before I knew who they were.

## You're the Right Mom For Your Kids

What happened right because of you today? I know I've asked you this before– and I'll probably ask you again in the future. We need to get better at giving ourselves credit. You are enough. You are worthy. You are valuable with or without productivity. You are important here on Earth, and I'm so glad you are here. You are exactly the right human to read this. Exactly the right woman. Exactly the right mom. Always and forever, exactly right.

# Mom Hacks:

When traveling with kids, always pack a spare outfit for yourself, too. In fact, leave it in the trunk 24/7.

When flu season hits, make a bin of crackers, ginger ale, and extra beach towels, just in case.

If possible, always make double meatballs. They freeze really well, and you'll have a backup when you need it.

Is the day falling apart? Just add water. Winter? Add a surprise toy at bath time. Summer/Spring/Fall: Try out buckets and paintbrushes so your kids can paint the walls outside or the sidewalk.

Send thank you cards any time of year to coaches, teachers, babysitters, and therapists who love your kids well.

Are you planning to run errands? Don't forget to bring extra snacks for yourself, too.

## You're the Right Mom For Your Kids

Can't tell whose towel is whose? Give everyone a color. Then you'll know which kid forgot and left theirs on the bathroom floor.

Bring out the bubbles. You can't be outraged and blow bubbles. Your kids can't either.

Tired? Let your kids drive cars on your body while lying on the couch or floor. Enjoy the free massage!

It's okay to lie down. Moms take breaks around the world. Siestas and tea times are popular for this reason.

Meal time challenge: If you must eat separately, stay with your kids while they eat. Sit and read your kids a book or listen to an audiobook or podcast at the table.

Summer Tip: Keep inexpensive flip-flops in the trunk in case your kids have a little too much fun in summer rain puddles.

Christy Thomas

Take care of Morning You: Start the dishwasher before bed if there are more than 8 dishes.
Set alarms on your phone to help yourself go to bed at a good hour. It would be best if you had sleep, too.

Create a morning playlist and dance with your kids in the morning before you leave the house.

Unfollow as often as needed on social media.

Send letters: Slow mail really deepens your friendships.

What got you here won't get you there. Expect to change things often in motherhood.

It's okay to wear laundry straight out of the basket.

Pipe cleaners in a pasta strainer make a fun kitchen toy.

Set alarms to practice talking to yourself kindly. I used one for years that said, "Breathe, this isn't an emergency."

Chalk-drawn obstacle courses are fun for ages 1-99.

## You're the Right Mom For Your Kids

Be "kindness ninjas" with your kids. Do random, stealthy acts of kindness for friends and neighbors together.

Picture books always stay in style. Grab some from the library to read aloud to your kids, regardless of age.

Take photos of flowers when walking with your kids. It will help you maintain the pace of someone who has shorter legs.

Selfies are perfect for moms because they help you stay in the photo with your kids.

Surprise your kids by asking them to teach you something you don't understand (and maybe don't value). Pokémon, video games, TV shows, and books are good places to start.

Try singing if you have no more words to say in a nice voice.

Feeling on edge? Puppets aren't just for kids. Find one and let your funny, impatient alter ego out.

It's okay if your kids sleep in tomorrow's clothes instead of pajamas.

We notice triggers quickly but miss the glimmers. Glimmers are tiny moments of joy. Look for them.

Develop your own favorite way to drink coffee. Create a calming ritual for yourself.

You are loved. You are loved. You are loved.

Ask your kids questions when you don't know what to do about something.

Hold the door for moms with kids younger than yours. You just made a big difference in their day.

You're the Right Mom For Your Kids

Thank you so much for reading this.

What I know for sure is that you have always been exactly the right, good enough mom for your kids. There are zero ways to be perfect and a million ways to be good enough.. In your highest joys of mothering and your lowest lows, I'm praying for you. You are loved and wanted and a drop-dead gorgeous miracle.

Always love and peace,

Christy Thomas

Christy Thomas

# Biography

Christy Thomas, the captivating podcaster behind "Keep Calm Mother On," shares her journey from a lonely, overwhelmed mother to a global motherhood mentor. Her dynamic storytelling and unwavering commitment to nurturing a supportive community have made her a beacon of strength and inspiration for countless parents.

To stay in touch, please check out the podcast Keep Calm Mother On.
www.ChristyThomasCoaching.com
@everyday_christy on Instagram
Youtube.com/@ChristyThomasCoaching
Play4life.christy@gmail.com

Made in United States
Troutdale, OR
12/07/2023

15516946R00106